RAT
COLORING BOOK

Get FREE printable coloring pages and discounted book prices sent straight to your e-mail inbox every week!

Sign up at:
www.adultcoloringworld.net

PREVIEWS:

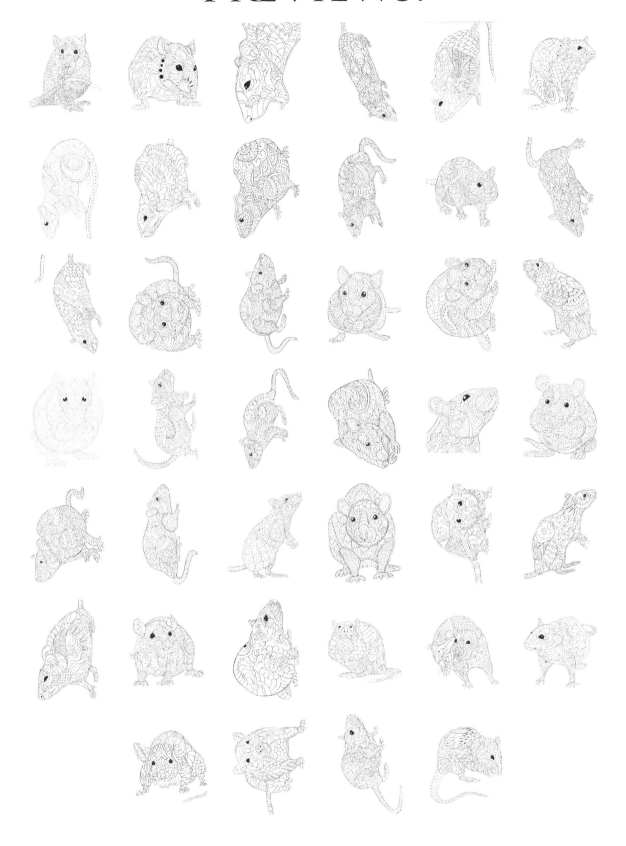

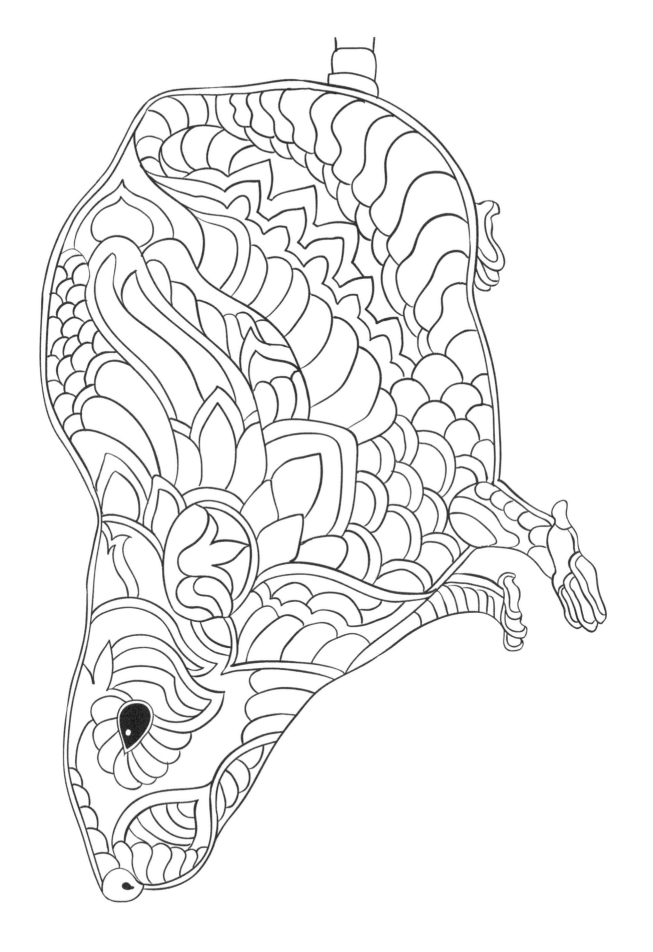

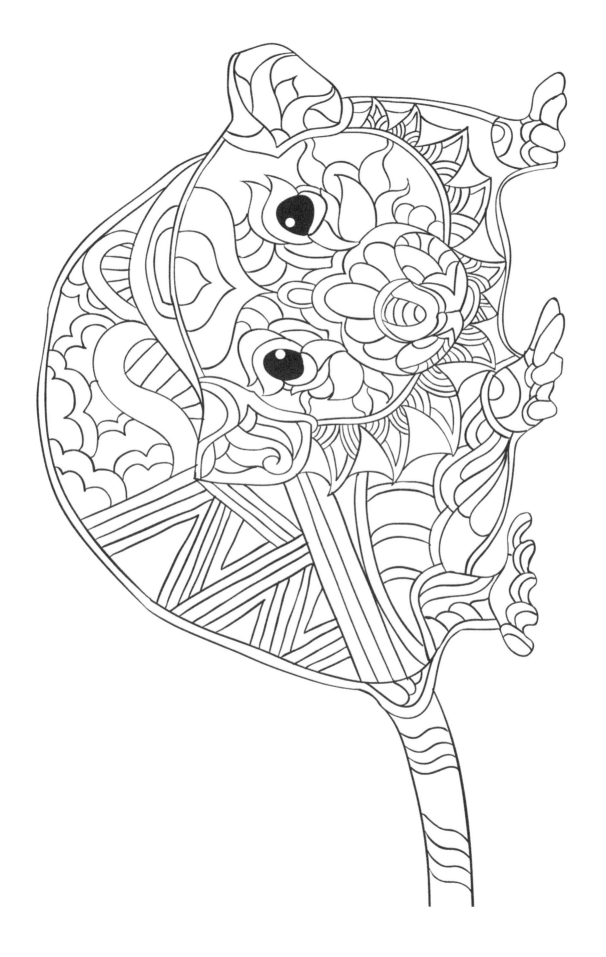

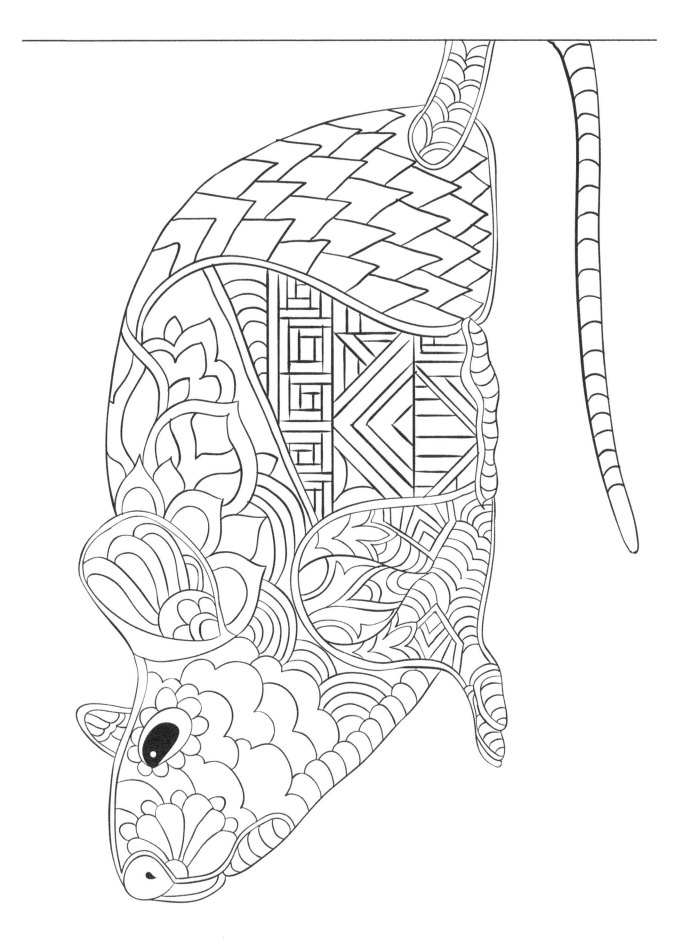

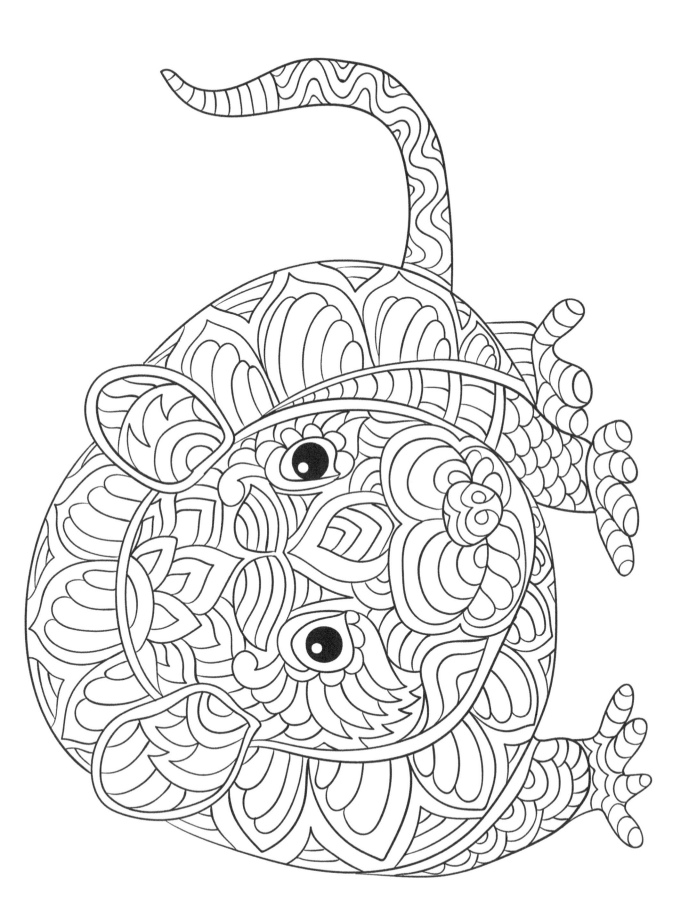

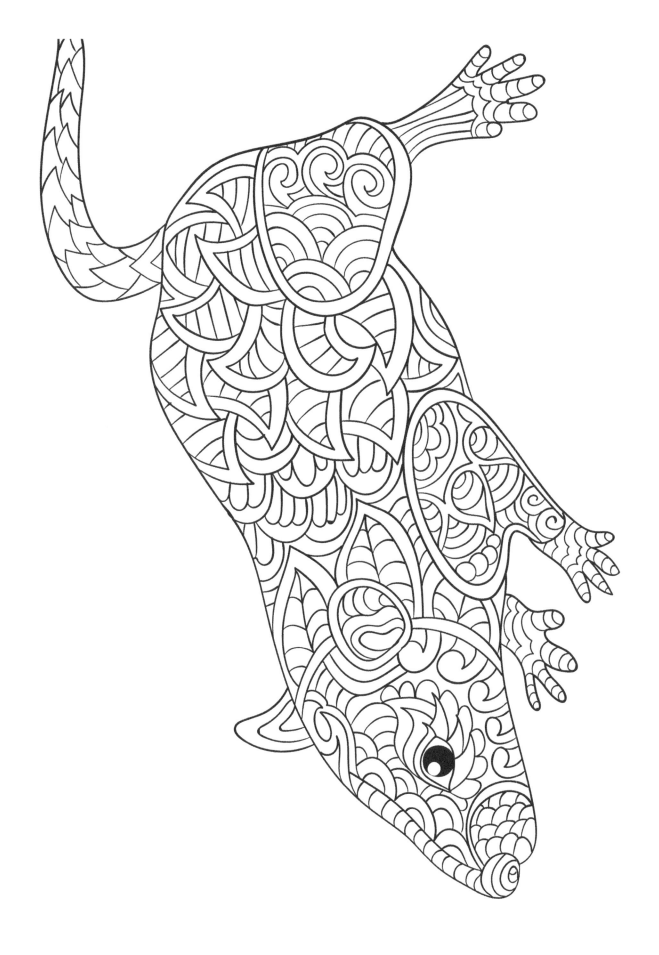

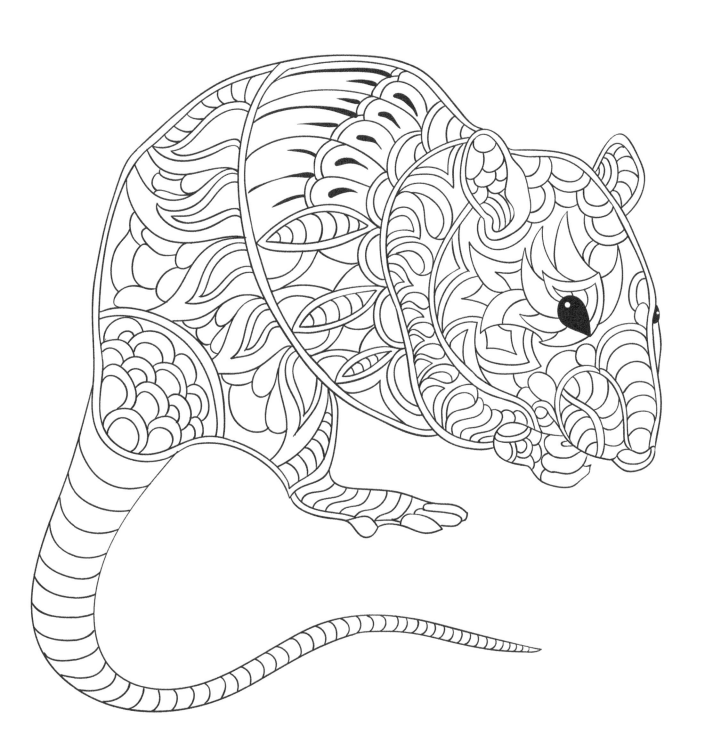

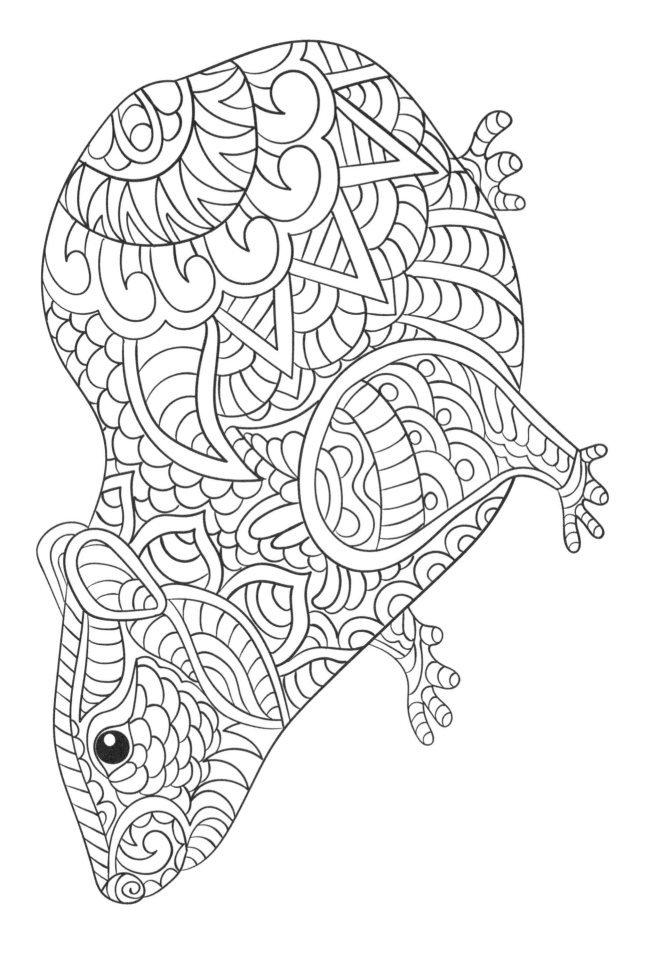

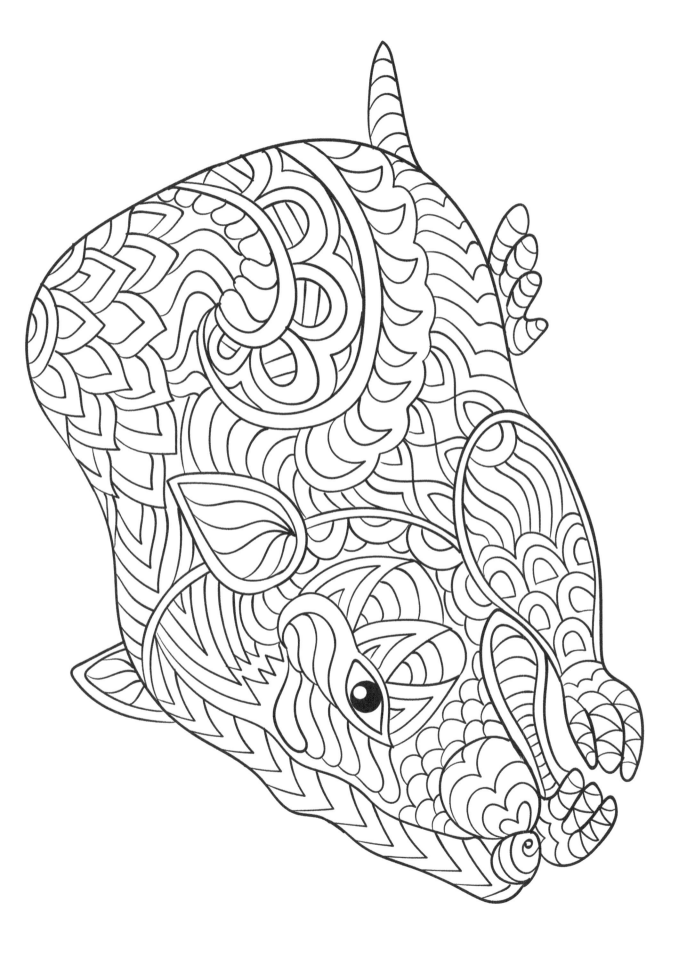

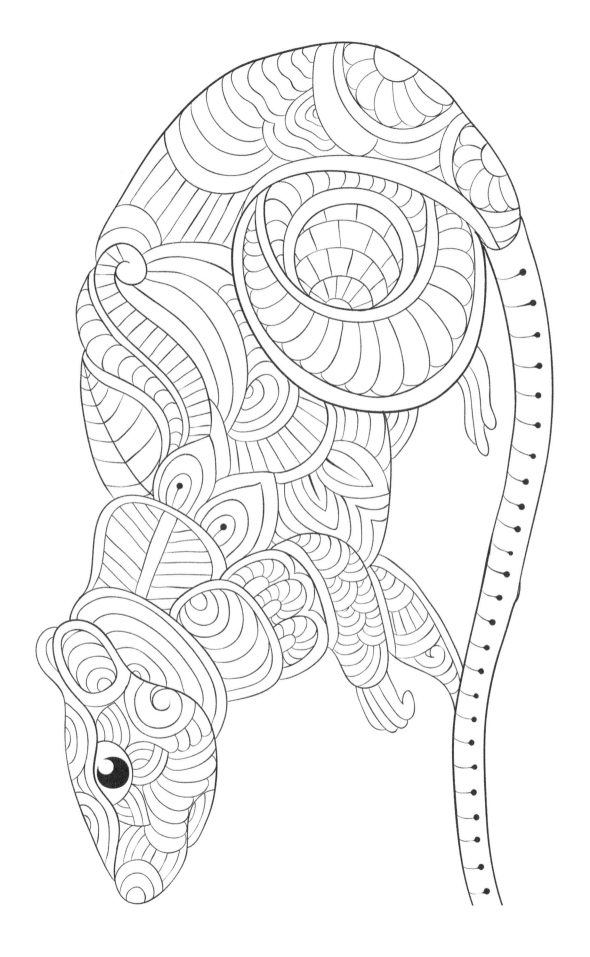

COLOR TEST PAGE

COLOR TEST PAGE

Made in the USA
Monee, IL
28 November 2022

18914201R00050